Houghton Mifflin

California Math

Circle Time

Student Book

- Circle Time
- Looking Ahead Activities

Visit **Education Place**
www.eduplace.com/kids

GRADE

K

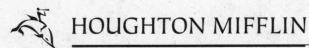

HOUGHTON MIFFLIN   BOSTON

ISBN 10: 0-547-17352-0
ISBN 13: 978-0-547-17352-8

11 12 0982 15 14 13 12
4500346521

Name _____

Top, Middle, Bottom

Problem of the Day ——————————— MG 2.2

Where is the teddy bear?
Where is the doll?

Measurement and Geometry ——————— MG 2.2

Place the cube on a desk.
Place the cube in your lap.
Place the cube in this box.

Calendar ——————————————————— MG 1.2

Numerical Fluency ——————————————— NS 1.2

1   2   3   4   5   6   7   8   9   10

Before, After, Between

Problem of the Day ——————————————— MG 2.2

Which object is on top?
on the bottom?
in the middle?

Measurement and Geometry ——————————— MG 2.2

Use position words to tell where
each shape is.

Calendar ——————————————————————— MG 1.3

Numerical Fluency ——————————————— NS 1.2

Inside, Outside

Problem of the Day ———————————————— MG 2.2

Which object is between the others?

Measurement and Geometry ———————————— MG 2.2

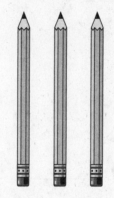

Word of the Day ————————————————————— MG 2.2

| after |

Which animal is after the rabbit? after the duck? after the cat?

Numerical Fluency ———————————————————— NS 1.2

Do we have five here?

Name _____

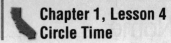

Left and Right

Problem of the Day ————————————————— MG 2.2

Which would you find inside a house?
Which would you find outside a house?

Measurement and Geometry ————————— MG 1.1

Which is longer? shorter?

Number of the Day ————————————————— NS 1.2

3

Numerical Fluency ————————————————— NS 1.2

Use with text pp. 10A–10D

Name _____

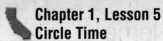
Act It Out

Problem of the Day ———————————————— MG 2.2

What is to the right of the house?
What is to the left?

Measurement and Geometry ———————————— MG 2.2

Draw a pencil on the left side.
Draw a crayon on the right side.

Number of the Day ———————————————— NS 1.2

5

Numerical Fluency ———————————————— NS 1.2

1   2   3   4   5   6   7   8   9   10

Same and Different

Problem of the Day ——————————————— MG 2.2

Name the opposites.

top
inside
left

Measurement and Geometry ——————————— MG 2.2

Place the counter to the right of the crayon.

Calendar ———————————————————— MG 1.2

Numerical Fluency ——————————————— NS 1.2

1, 2, 3, 4, 5, 6, 7, 8, 9, 10, 9, 8, 7, 6, 5, 4, 3, 2, 1

Name _____

Sort by Color

Problem of the Day ———————————— KEY **AF 1.1**

How are these things the same and
how are they different?

Measurement and Geometry ———————— MG 2.2

Words of the Day ———————————————— MG 2.2

right	left

Numerical Fluency ———————————————— NS 1.2

7
Use with text pp. 19A–20

Name _____

Sort by Size

Problem of the Day ———————————— AF 1.0

Name as many things as you can that are red.

Algebra and Functions ———————————— KEY AF 1.1

How are the markers the same?
How are they different?

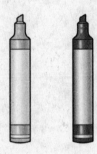

Number of the Day ———————————— NS 1.2

10

What else are there ten of?

Numerical Fluency ———————————— NS 1.2

8
Use with text pp. 21A–22

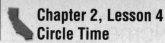
Sort by Shape

Problem of the Day ———————————— AF 1.0

How are these animals the same?
How are they different?

Measurement and Geometry ———————— MG 1.1

Words of the Day ————————————— MG 2.2

same	different

Numerical Fluency ———————————— NS 1.2

3 9 1
6
2
4
8 5
7

Name _____

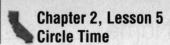
Logical Thinking

Problem of the Day ———————————————— AF 1.0

What are two ways you could sort the shapes?

Measurement and Geometry ———————— MG 2.2

Which are the same?
How are the circles different?

Words of the Day ———————————————— MG 2.2

top	bottom

Numerical Fluency ———————————————— NS 1.2

3

8   9   6   4   5   7

10   2

Some, All, and None

Problem of the Day ———————————— KEY **AF 1.1**

How can you sort these buttons?
In what other way might you sort them?

Measurement and Geometry ———————— MG 2.2

Draw a tree to the right of your house.
Draw a puppy to the left of your house.

Calendar ————————————————————— MG 2.2

Numerical Fluency ————————————— NS 1.2

11

Graph With Real Objects

Problem of the Day ———————————————— KEY AF 1.1

Which toys would you put in a
box that has all teddy bears?
some teddy bears?
no teddy bears?

Measurement and Geometry ———————————— MG 2.2

Which object is inside the box?
to the right of the box?

Number of the Day ——————————————————— NS 1.2

5

Numerical Fluency ——————————————————— NS 1.2

1 2 3 4 5 6 7 8 9 10 11 12 13 14 15 16 17 18 19 20

Use with text pp. 30E–30H

Name _____

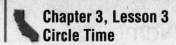
Sort and Graph Coins

Problem of the Day ———————————— SDAP 1.1

Make a real graph to show these counters.
Which color has more?

Algebra and Functions ———————————— KEY AF 1.1

Sort by shape.
Sort by color.

Word of the Day ———————————— MG 2.2

between

Numerical Fluency ———————————— NS 1.2

Name _____

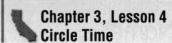

Picture Graphs

Problem of the Day ————————————————— KEY **AF 1.1**

How would you sort these coins to make a graph?
Which row would have more items?

Measurement and Geometry ———————————— MG 2.2

Which toy is between? Which toy is on the right? the left?

Number of the Day ———————————————————— NS 1.2

2

Numerical Fluency ————————————————————— NS 1.2

14

Use with text pp. 33A–34

Name _____

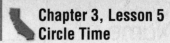
Make a Graph

Problem of the Day ————————————— SDAP 1.1

Which is the favorite ball game to play?

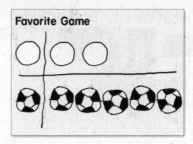

Algebra and Functions ————————————— KEY **AF 1.1**

Words of the Day ————————————— MG 2.2

| before | after |

Numerical Fluency ————————————— NS 1.2

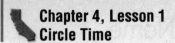
Sort Plane Shapes

Problem of the Day ———————————————— SDAP 1.1

What do the most children like to play with?

What We Like To Play With

Statistics, Data Analysis, and Probability ———————— KEY SDAP 1.2

Calendar ————————————————————————— MG 1.3

Numerical Fluency ———————————————————— NS 1.2

Are there 20, more than 20, or less than 20?

Circle Time
16
Use with text pp. 49A–50

Name _____

Circle or Square

Problem of the Day ———————————— MG 2.1

Which two shapes have the same number of sides?
How many sides do they each have?

Measurement and Geometry ——————— KEY **MG 1.0**

Which is shorter, the door or the chair? the door or the children?

Word of the Day ————————————— MG 2.0

shape

Numerical Fluency ———————————— NS 1.2

Name _____

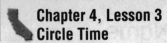
Rectangle or Triangle

Problem of the Day ———————————— NS 1.2

How many circles do you see?

Measurement and Geometry ———————— MG 2.2

Number of the Day ———————————— NS 1.2

Numerical Fluency ———————————— NS 1.3

Does it show 3?
If not, should I add dots or erase dots?

Name _____

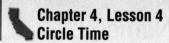
Draw a Picture

Problem of the Day ——————————————— MG 2.1

It is not round.
It has three straight sides.
Which shape is it?

Number Sense ——————————————— NS 1.3

Number of the Day ——————————————— MG 2.0

What things have 4 sides?

Numerical Fluency ——————————————— NS 1.2

Find a partner and take turns counting.

Name _____

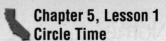
Rhythmic Patterns

Problem of the Day ———————————————— MR 2.1

Draw a shape with more sides than the shape below.
Name the shape you drew.

Algebra and Functions ———————————— KEY **AF 1.1**

Which one does not belong?
Draw it on your mat.

Calendar ———————————————————— MG 2.2

Is today's date in the top week, the bottom week, or in one of the
weeks in the middle of the calendar?

Numerical Fluency ———————————————— NS 1.1

Color Patterns

Problem of the Day ———————————— KEY SDAP 1.2

Follow the pattern.

Jump once. Clap once.
Jump once. Clap once.

Continue the pattern.

Algebra and Functions ———————————— KEY AF 1.1

Words of the Day ———————————— MG 2.2

big	small

Numerical Fluency ———————————— NS 1.2

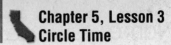
Size Patterns

Problem of the Day ———————————— KEY SDAP 1.2

What color is likely to come next in the pattern?

Measurement and Geometry ———————— MG 2.1

Number of the Day ———————————— NS 1.2

Numerical Fluency ———————————— NS 1.2

Use with text pp. 63A–64

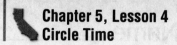

Patterns with Plane Shapes

Problem of the Day ————————————

What comes next?

Algebra and Functions ————————————

Words of the Day ————————————

inside	outside

Numerical Fluency ————————————

Are there four?

If not, should we draw more or erase some to make four?

Find a Pattern

Problem of the Day ——————————————— KEY SDAP 1.2

Jen will put down the shape that comes next.
Which shape will she put down?

Statistics, Data Analysis, and Probability ——————— KEY SDAP 1.2

What letters name the pattern?

Word of the Day ——————————————————— SDAP 1.0

some

Numerical Fluency ——————————————————— NS 1.2

Patterns and Positions

Problem of the Day ——————————— KEY SDAP 1.2

What part of this pattern repeats?
What letters describe the pattern?

Measurement and Geometry ——————————— MG 2.2

Number of the Day ——————————— NS 1.1

4

Numerical Fluency ——————————— NS 1.2

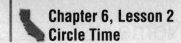
Patterns That Are the Same

Problem of the Day ———————————— KEY **SDAP 1.2**

Act out the pattern below.
Show what position is likely to come next.

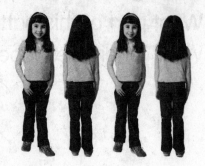

Algebra and Functions ———————————— KEY **AF 1.1**

Calendar ————————————————— MG 1.2

Numerical Fluency ——————————————— NS 1.2

Name _____

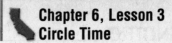

Make Patterns

Problem of the Day

KEY

How can you show the same pattern as a color pattern?

Measurement and Geometry

MG 2.0

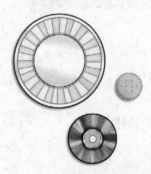

Word of the Day

NS 1.2

none

Numerical Fluency

NS 1.1

Count with teamwork.

Name _____

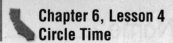

Find a Pattern

Problem of the Day ———————————— KEY **SDAP 1.2**

Use these shapes to draw your own pattern.
You may repeat each shape.

Statistics, Data Analysis, and Probability ———————— KEY **SDAP 1.2**

Calendar ————————————————————— NS 1.1

Count the Mondays this month.
Count the Tuesdays.
Are there more, fewer, or the same number
of Mondays as Tuesdays?

Numerical Fluency ————————————————— NS 1.2

How many groups of 3 children can we make?

Circle Time
28
Use with text pp. 79A–80

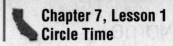
One-to-One Correspondence

Problem of the Day ———————————————— KEY SDAP 1.2

What group is likely to come next?

Statistics, Data Analysis, and Probability ——————————— KEY SDAP 1.2

What is likely to come next in this pattern?

Calendar ———————————————————— MG 1.3

Numerical Fluency ——————————————— NS 1.2

Circle Time

29

Use with text pp. 92A–92D

Name _____

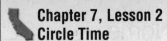
Equal Sets

Problem of the Day ——————————— NS 1.1

Will every pail get a shovel? Tell why.

Measurement and Geometry ——————— MG 2.2

Word of the Day ——————————— KEY SDAP 1.2

| pattern |

Numerical Fluency ——————————— NS 1.2

If one more has arms raised, how many will have arms down?

Name _____

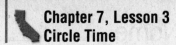
More

Problem of the Day ———————————— NS 1.1

Which sets have the same number?

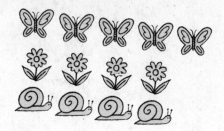

Measurement and Geometry ———————— KEY MG 1.0

Name a room in the school that is larger than the classroom.

Words of the Day ———————————— AF 1.0

same	different

Numerical Fluency ———————————— NS 1.2

Find the number 5!

31

Use with text pp. 95A–96

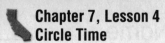
Less

Problem of the Day ——————————————— NS 1.1

Which set has more?

Statistics, Data Analysis, and Probability ——————— KEY SDAP 1.2

What letters name the pattern?

Words of the Day ——————————————— MG 2.2

before	after

between

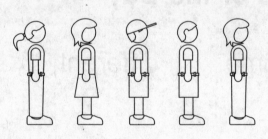

Numerical Fluency ——————————————— NS 1.1

Circle Time

32

Use with text pp. 97A–98

Name _____

Draw a Picture

Problem of the Day ———————————— NS 1.1

Are there fewer stars or fewer circles?

Algebra and Functions ———————————— KEY AF 1.1

How are they the same? different?

Number of the Day ———————————— NS 1.1

2

What other things come in twos?

Numerical Fluency ———————————— NS 1.2

Count and Read Numbers 1–3

Problem of the Day ———————————— NS 1.1

Count the dogs. Draw a picture to show more cats than dogs.

Number Sense Review ———————————— NS 1.2

Word of the Day ———————————— KEY SDAP 1.2

pattern

Numerical Fluency ———————————— NS 1.2

1 2 3 4 5 6 7 8 9 10 11 12 13 14 15 16 17 18 19 20

34

Use with text pp. 104A–104D

Name _____

One and Two

Problem of the Day ⎯⎯⎯⎯⎯⎯⎯⎯⎯⎯⎯⎯⎯⎯ NS 1.2

What numbers do you see?
What number comes next?

1 2

Number Sense Review ⎯⎯⎯⎯⎯⎯⎯⎯⎯⎯⎯⎯ NS 1.1

Which set has more? fewer?

Calendar ⎯⎯⎯⎯⎯⎯⎯⎯⎯⎯⎯⎯⎯⎯⎯⎯⎯⎯⎯ MG 1.2

Numerical Fluency ⎯⎯⎯⎯⎯⎯⎯⎯⎯⎯⎯⎯ NS 1.2

Circle Time

35

Use with text pp. 105A–106

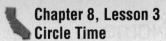
Three

Problem of the Day ——————— NS 1.2

Which picture shows one?
Which picture shows two?

Number Sense Review ——————— NS 1.2

Word of the Day ——————— NS 1.1

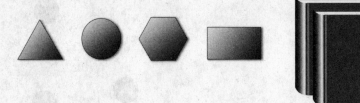

more

Numerical Fluency ——————— KEY **AF 1.1**

How many are in each group?

Name _____

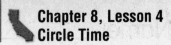

Numbers 1–3

Problem of the Day ———————————— NS 1.2

Draw the same number of ducks as you see here.

Algebra and Functions Review ———— KEY **AF 1.1**

Words of the Day ———————————— MG 2.2

bigger	smaller

Numerical Fluency ———————————— NS 1.2

1 2 3 4 5 6 7 8 9 10 11 12 13 14 15 16 17 18 19 20

Name _____

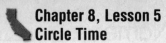

Use a Graph

Problem of the Day ———————————— NS 1.2

How many stars?
How many hearts?
How many flowers?

Measurement and Geometry Review ——— MG 1.2

Would you most likely drink a glass of milk
at lunch time or math time?

Number of the Day ———————————— NS 1.2

3

What groups of 3 can you name?

Numerical Fluency ———————————— NS 1.2

5   10   2   9   8   3   6   7   4

Name _____

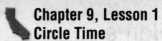

Four

Problem of the Day ———————————————— NS 1.2

Draw a picture to show one carrot for each rabbit.

Statistics, Data Analysis, and Probability ———————— KEY SDAP 1.2

Number of the Day ———————————————— NS 1.2

Numerical Fluency ———————————————— NS 1.2

Five

Problem of the Day ———————————— NS 1.1

Draw a group with one more apple.
How many apples did you draw?

Statistics, Data Analysis, and Probability ———— KEY SDAP 1.2

What will most likely come next?

Word of the Day ———————————————— NS 1.1

fewer

Numerical Fluency ————————————————— NS 1.2

4 0 8 3 2 7 6 9 1 5

Circle Time

40

Use with text pp. 119A–120

Name _____

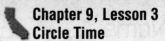

Zero

Problem of the Day ——————————— NS 1.1

What number tells how many?

Number Sense ——————————— NS 1.2

Word of the Day ——————————— NS 1.1

match one to one

Numerical Fluency ——————————— NS 1.2

Which group has more?

Name _____

Numbers 0–5

Problem of the Day ———————————— NS 1.2

Count to 4.
Did you say the number 3?
Did you say the number 5?

Measurement and Geometry ———————— MG 1.1

Name something that is lighter than your book bag.

Calendar ————————————————————— MG 1.2

Numerical Fluency ———————————————— NS 1.2

Are there 20, more than 20, or fewer than 20?

Name _____

Use a Picture

Problem of the Day ————————————————— MG 2.2

Which animal is before the dog?
Which animal is after the dog?

Number Sense ——————————————————— NS 1.1

_____ is more than _____.

Calendar ——————————————————————— MG 1.2

Numerical Fluency ————————————————— NS 1.2

2 0 4 3 1 5

Name _____

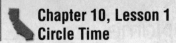

Hands On: Count and Read Numbers 1–7

Problem of the Day ———————————— NS 1.1

Which set has the largest number?

Measurement and Geometry ———————— MG 1.2

Word of the Day ———————————————— MG 2.1

rectangle

Numerical Fluency ———————————————— NS 1.2

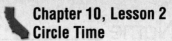
Hands On: Six

Problem of the Day —————————— NS 1.2

Tim says 1.

Then he says 1, 2.

Then he says 1, 2, 3.

Then he says 1, 2, 3, 4.

What is Tim likely to say next?

Measurement and Geometry ———— MG 2.0

I spy a paper.

It is a rectangle.

Calendar ————————————— MG 1.3

Sunday	Monday	Tuesday	Wednesday	Thursday	Friday	Saturday

Numerical Fluency ——————— NS 1.2

Are there 20 here today? more? fewer?

Hands On: Seven

Problem of the Day —————————————— NS 1.1

Draw a group that has one more.
How many does your new group have?

Measurement and Geometry ——————— MG 1.1

Word of the Day ———————————————— MG 2.2

circle

What is the same about the shapes?
What is different?

Numerical Fluency ———————————————— NS 1.2

4   8   5   14

10   2

15   13

7

3   12

1   9

6

11

Name _____

Show Parts 3–7

Problem of the Day ———————————— NS 1.1

Which group has more?
How many more?

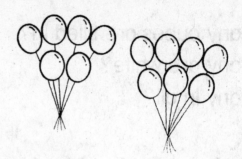

Statistics, Data Analysis, and Probability ———————————— SDAP 1.1

Which row has most?

Number of the Day ———————————— NS 1.2

Numerical Fluency ———————————— NS 1.2

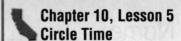
Problem Solving: Look for a Pattern

Problem of the Day

How many cubes are filled in?
How many are white?
How many in all?

Statistics, Data Analysis, and Probability ———————————— SDAP 1.1

Are there more sunny days or cloudy days?

Number of the Day ———————————— NS 1.1

7

Will there be 7, more, or fewer when we line up today?

Numerical Fluency ———————————— NS 1.2

2 5 1 8
6 0 4 3
9 7

Name _____

Eight

Problem of the Day ———————————— NS 1.1

Which group has more?
How many more?

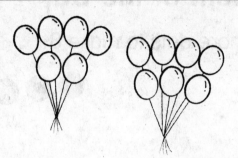

Statistics, Data Analysis, and Probability ———————— SDAP 1.1

Which row has more?

Number of the Day ———————————— NS 1.2

8

Numerical Fluency ———————————— NS 1.2

4 7 2 0 6 I 3 5

Name _____

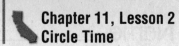
Nine

Problem of the Day ——————————— NS 1.3

Draw more dots to make 8.

Measurement and Geometry ——————— KEY

How can we compare the ribbon?

Number of the Day ——————————— NS 1.3

8

Which set shows more?
Which number is larger?

Numerical Fluency ——————————— NS 1.2

Ten

Problem of the Day ————————————————— NS 1.1

Sam has nine crayons.
Tina has seven crayons.
Who has more?

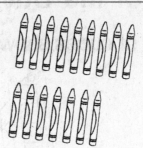

Measurement and Geometry ————————— MG 1.2

Which would you do in the evening, have dinner
or have breakfast?

Calendar ——————————————————————— MG 1.2

Numerical Fluency ———————————————— NS 1.2

Form groups of 4 or 5 students.

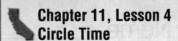
Show Parts 8–10

Problem of the Day ———————————————— KEY **NS 1.0**

Which group of cubes shows 10?

Algebra and Functions ———————————————— KEY **AF 1.1**

Word of the Day ———————————————— MG 2.2

all

Tell about the bears.
Use the word <u>all</u>.

Numerical Fluency ———————————————— NS 1.2

What number comes before 6 when we count? after 8?

Circle Time

52

Use with text pp. 154A–154D

Use a Picture

Problem of the Day KEY NS 1.0

How many circles do you see?
How many are black?
How many are white?

Algebra and Functions KEY AF 1.1

Which cube does not belong? Why?

Word of the Day MG 2.1

triangle

How many sides does a triangle have?

Numerical Fluency NS 1.3

Which hand shows the larger number of fingers?

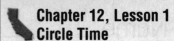
Sort by Number

Problem of the Day ——————————— KEY **NS 1.0**

What number does the picture show?
What are the parts?

Number Sense ————————————————— NS 1.2

1   2   3   4   5

Calendar ————————————————— KEY **NS 1.0**

Numerical Fluency ———————————————— NS 1.2

20 21 22 23 24 25 26 27 28 29 30

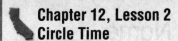
Order Numbers to 10

Problem of the Day ———————————— NS 1.2

What number does this picture show?

Statistics, Data Analysis, and Probability ———————— KEY **SDAP 1.2**

Word of the Day ———————————— KEY **SDAP 1.2**

| pattern |

Numerical Fluency ———————————— NS 1.2

Name _____

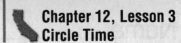
More and Less

Problem of the Day ———————————————— NS 1.2

I am thinking of a number.
The number comes before 9.
It comes after 7.
What is the number?

7   9

Statistics, Data Analysis, and Probability ———————— SDAP 1.1

Number of the Day ———————————————— KEY NS 1.0

9

Numerical Fluency ———————————————— NS 1.2

Use with text pp. 165A–166

Name _____

Ordinal Numbers

Problem of the Day ——————————————— NS 1.3

Draw more circles until there
are more circles than stars.

Measurement and Geometry ——————————— MG 1.1

Which holds more?

Calendar ————————————————————————— NS 1.1

Numerical Fluency ————————————————— NS 1.2

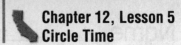
Use a Graph

Problem of the Day ——————————— NS 1.2

Which animal is the sixth in line?

Number Sense ——————————— NS 1.2

3 6 1 7 0 9 2 10 4 8 5

Words of the Day ——————————— NS 1.1

| more | less |

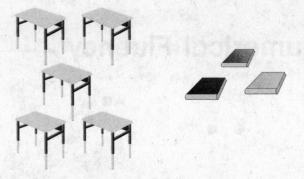

Numerical Fluency ——————————— NS 1.2

2   4   6   8   10   12   14   16   18   20   22   24   26   28   30

Name _____

Model Addition

Problem of the Day ———————————— SDAP 1.1

Use a graph to show how many in each group of shapes.

Number Sense ——————————————————— NS 1.2

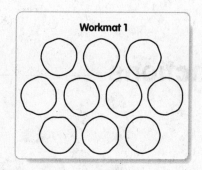

Calendar ———————————————————————— NS 1.2

Numerical Fluency ——————————————— NS 1.1

Name _____

Add with Cubes

Problem of the Day —————————— NS 2.0

How many bees are there in all?

Algebra and Functions ———————— KEY AF 1.1

Word of the Day ——————————— NS 1.2

| tenth |

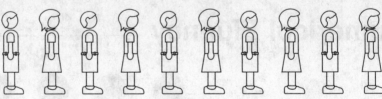

Numerical Fluency ————————— NS 1.2

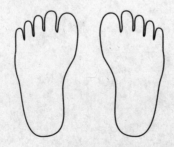

Name _____

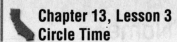
Addition Stories

Problem of the Day —————————————— KEY NS 2.1

Use cubes. Tell how many frogs in all.

Measurement and Geometry ———————————— MG 1.2

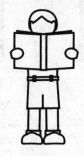

Words of the Day —————————————————— MG 2.2

right	left

Numerical Fluency —————————————————— NS 1.2

1 2 3 4 5

Name _____

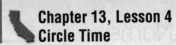
Use Pictures to Add

Problem of the Day ———————————— NS 2.0

Use this picture to tell an addition
story about birds.

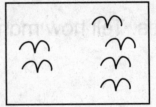

Number Sense Review ———————————— NS 1.2

Number of the Day ———————————— NS 1.1

Numerical Fluency ———————————— NS 1.2

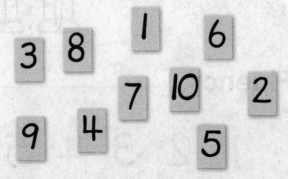

Name _____

Use a Picture

Problem of the Day ———————————— KEY

Which group shows 6 marbles and one more?

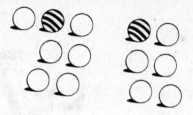

Statistics, Data Analysis, and Probability ———————— KEY

Calendar ———————————————————— NS 1.2

Numerical Fluency ————————————————— NS 1.2

When we count, what number is between 12 and 14?
What numbers are between 7 and 10?

Name _____

Model Subtraction

Problem of the Day ————————————— NS 2.0

Which numbers tell the story?

_____ and _____ _____ in all

Number Sense ————————————— NS 1.1

Are there more chairs or children?

Calendar ————————————— NS 1.2

Is today the first, second, third, fourth, or
fifth day of the school week?

Numerical Fluency ————————————— NS 1.1

Name _____

Subtract with Cubes

Problem of the Day ———————————— NS 2.0

How can you make this group have fewer blocks?

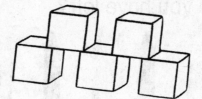

Number Sense ———————————————— NS 1.2

first, second, _____, fourth, _____, sixth,
seventh, _____, ninth, _____.

Word of the Day ——————————————— NS 1.1

first

Numerical Fluency ————————————— NS 1.2

Name _____

Subtraction Stories

Problem of the Day ———————————— NS 2.0

You have 5 crayons. You give 1 to your friend.
How many crayons do you have left?

Algebra and Functions ———————————— KEY AF 1.1

If you sort by size, which one does not belong?

Word of the Day ———————————— MG 2.1

I have four sides.
I have four corners.
All my sides are equal.
What am I?

Numerical Fluency ———————————— NS 1.2

60 61 62 63 64 65 66 67 68 69 70

Use Pictures to Subtract

Problem of the Day ———————————— NS 2.0

How many squirrels are left?

Measurement and Geometry ———————— MG 2.1

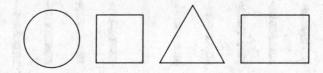

Number of the Day ————————————— NS 1.2

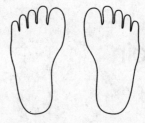

Numerical Fluency ———————————— KEY NS 1.0

Name _____

Draw a Picture

Problem of the Day ———————————— KEY NS 2.1

Will the number of rabbits be one more or one less?
How do you know?

Number Sense ———————————— NS 1.2

Word of the Day ———————————— KEY NS 1.0

join

j - o - i - n

Numerical Fluency ———————————— NS 1.2

35, 36, 37, 38, 39, 40

Join Parts

Problem of the Day ———————— KEY NS 2.1

There are 7 birds in a tree.
Then 2 birds leave.
How many birds are left?

Statistics, Data Analysis, and Probability ———— SDAP 1.1

Which row has more? less?

Calendar ———————————————— MG 1.2

Numerical Fluency ———————————— NS 1.2

Name _____

Separate Parts

Problem of the Day _____ KEY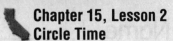

Which picture shows 4 + 3 = 7?

Number Sense _____ NS 2.0

$$\_ + \_\_ = \_\_$$

Word of the Day _____ NS 2.0

separate    s-e-p-a-r-a-t-e

Numerical Fluency _____ NS 1.2

30 29 28 27 26 25 24 23 22 21 20

70   Use with text pp. 215A–216

Addition and Subtraction Problems

Problem of the Day

Which group shows 3 − 1 bananas?

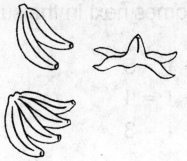

Number Sense

How could I share this eight-cube train with a friend? How do I
know the parts are equal?

Words of the Day

equal sets

Numerical Fluency

Is it more than 10, less, or the same?

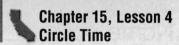
Relate Addition and Subtraction

Problem of the Day ———————————— NS 2.0

What comes next in the subtraction pattern?

$6 - 1 = 5$
$5 - 1 = 4$
$4 - 1 = 3$

Measurement and Geometry ———————— MG 1.1

Which would hold more, a cup or a teaspoon? Which would hold less, a cup or a wastebasket?

Number of the Day ———————————— NS 1.2

Numerical Fluency ———————————— NS 1.1

0 13 12 14
19 7 5 9 16
6 17 18 11
4 10 15
2 8 1 3

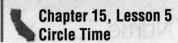
Act It Out

Problem of the Day ———————————— NS 2.0

What number can you write to complete both
number sentences?

$$8 - 2 = \underline{\quad}$$
$$\underline{\quad} + 2 = 8$$

Statistics, Data Analysis, and Probability ———————— SDAP 1.1

Which color is the favorite?

Word of the Day ———————————————— NS 1.2

Numerical Fluency ——————————————— NS 1.2

4   10   16   7   2   15   12   20   9   6   1   8   19   11   14   18   5   3   13   17

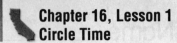
Record Addition

Problem of the Day ——————————— KEY NS 2.1

You have 7 pennies.
You get 2 more pennies.
You take away 2 pennies.

How many pennies do you have in all?

Algebra and Functions ——————————— KEY AF 1.1

Calendar ——————————————— KEY NS 2.1

July						
Sun.	Mon.	Tue.	Wed.	Thu.	Fri.	Sat.
			1	2	3	4
5	6	7	8	9	10	11
12	13	14	15	16	17	18
19	20	21	22	23	24	25
26	27	28	29	30	31	

August						
Sun.	Mon.	Tue.	Wed.	Thu.	Fri.	Sat.
			1	2	3	4
5	6	7	8	9	10	11
12	13	14	15	16	17	18
19	20	21	22	23	24	25
26	27	28	29	30	31	

September						
Sun.	Mon.	Tue.	Wed.	Thu.	Fri.	Sat.
			1	2	3	4
5	6	7	8	9	10	11
12	13	14	15	16	17	18
19	20	21	22	23	24	25
26	27	28	29	30		

October						
Sun.	Mon.	Tue.	Wed.	Thu.	Fri.	Sat.
			1	2	3	4
5	6	7	8	9	10	11
12	13	14	15	16	17	18
19	20	21	22	23	24	25
26	27	28	29	30	31	

November						
Sun.	Mon.	Tue.	Wed.	Thu.	Fri.	Sat.
			1	2	3	4
5	6	7	8	9	10	11
12	13	14	15	16	17	18
19	20	21	22	23	24	25
26	27	28	29	30		

December						
Sun.	Mon.	Tue.	Wed.	Thu.	Fri.	Sat.
			1	2	3	4
5	6	7	8	9	10	11
12	13	14	15	16	17	18
19	20	21	22	23	24	25
26	27	28	29	30	31	

Numerical Fluency ——————————— NS 1.2

9 8 10 7 6

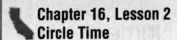
Record Subtraction

Problem of the Day ———————————— NS 2.0

What number sentence shows how many butterflies in all?

Number Sense ———————————— NS 1.0

Word of the Day ———————————— NS 1.1

equal	 

Numerical Fluency ———————————— NS 1.2

1 2 3 4 5 6 7 8 9 10 11 12 13 14 15

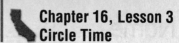
Add 1 or 2

Problem of the Day ———————————— KEY **NS 2.1**

Which shows the number sentence 6 − 5 = 1?

Measurement and Geometry ——————————— MG 2.2

Calendar ————————————————————— NS 2.0

Numerical Fluency ——————————————— NS 1.1

Name _____

Subtract 1 or 2

Problem of the Day ———————————————— KEY NS 2.1

If two more ants join this group,
how many ants will there be in all?

Number Sense ———————————————————— NS 1.2

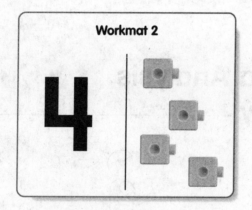

Workmat 2

Number of the Day ——————————————————— NS 1.2

How many are wearing purple?

Numerical Fluency ——————————————————— NS 1.2

Start at 3, count on 2 more.

77
Use with text pp. 229A–230

Name _____

Use a Picture

Problem of the Day —————————————— NS 2.0

If two dragonflies fly away, how many will be left?

Statistics, Data Analysis and Probability —————— KEY SDAP 1.2

Words of the Day ——————————————— NS 2.0

| number sentence |

Numerical Fluency ——————————————— NS 1.2

What are two numbers before 16? What is one number before 12?

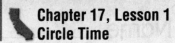
Numbers 10–19

Problem of the Day ————————————— MR 1.2

June saw 9 flies on a picnic blanket. 7 flew away. How many were left?

Number Sense ————————————————— NS 1.2

Calendar ————————————————————— MG 1.2

Numerical Fluency ——————————————— NS 1.2

1 2 3 4 5 6 7 8 9 10 11 12 13 14 15 16 17 18 19 20 21 22 23 24 25 26 27 28 29 30

Circle Time
79
Use with text pp. 244A–244

Name _____

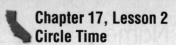
Numbers 10–12

Problem of the Day —————————————— NS 1.2

Count. What numbers are missing?

10, 11, ____, 13, 14, ____

Algebra and Functions —————————— KEY

In which two ways could they be sorted?

Number of the Day —————————————— NS 1.1

Name a number less than 10; greater than 10.

Numerical Fluency —————————————— NS 1.2

1 2 3 4 5 6 7 8 9 10 11 12 13 14 15 16 17 18 19 20 21 22 23 24 25 26 27 28 29 30

Name _____

Numbers 13–15

Problem of the Day ———————————— NS 1.2

Which group has more than 10 and less than 12?

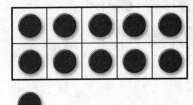 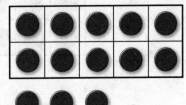

Measurement and Geometry ———————— MG 1.1

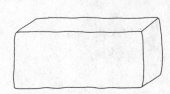 

Word of the Day ———————————————— NS 2.0

total

Numerical Fluency ———————————————— NS 3.1

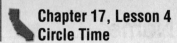
Numbers 16–19

Problem of the Day ——————————— NS 1.2

How many more counters make 15?

Measurement and Geometry ——————— MG 1.1

Word of the Day ——————————————— NS 2.0

| subtract |

If you wanted to find out how many crackers you would have left
if you gave some to a friend, would you add or subtract?

Numerical Fluency ——————————————— NS 1.2

15 2 19
3   8 14 9 6
18 11
5 7 13
4 17 16
12   10 3 20

Use a Graph

Problem of the Day ——————————————— NS 1.2

What is the missing number?

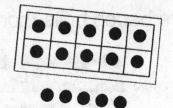

10 and ___ more is 15.

Measurement and Geometry ——————— MG 1.2

What things do we usually do in the morning at school? in the afternoon?

Calendar ——————————————————————— MG 1.2

How many Wednesdays are in this month? What was yesterday's day and date?

Numerical Fluency ——————————————— NS 1.3

Use with text pp. 251A–252

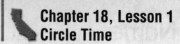
Hands On: Show Parts 11-14

Problem of the Day —————————————— SDAP 1.1

How many more beach balls than shovels are for sale?

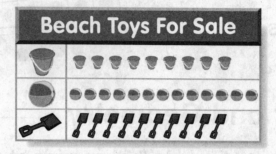

Number Sense —————————————————— NS 2.0

6 + 2 = 8

Calendar ———————————————————————— NS 1.2

How are these numbers like 1, 2, 3, and 4? How are they different?

Numerical Fluency ———————————————— NS 1.1

Circle Time

84

Use with text pp. 257A-258

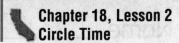
Hands On: Show Parts 15–19

Problem of the Day KEY **NS 1.0**

What are two different ways to show 11 in two parts?

Algebra and Functions KEY **AF 1.1**

Which fish does not belong? Why?

Word of the Day ——————————————————— MG 2.1

square

Numerical Fluency ——————————————————— NS 2.1

7   14

Circle Time

85

Use with text pp. 259A–260

Order Numbers Through 19

Problem of the Day ——————————————— KEY NS 1.0

Here is one way to show parts for 15:

How can you show parts for 15 in a different way?

Measurement and Geometry ——————————— MG 2.1

Number of the Day ——————————————— NS 1.2

19

Numerical Fluency ——————————————— KEY NS 1.0

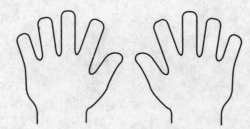

Name _____

Estimate Quantities Through 19

Problem of the Day ———————————————— NS 1.2

The house numbers are in order. What is the number on the house with the opened door?

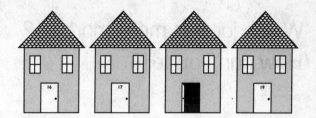

Number Sense ———————————————— KEY NS 2.1

Calendar ———————————————— NS 3.1

Numerical Fluency ———————————————— NS 1.2

10	11	12

Name _____

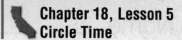

Problem Solving: Guess and Check

Problem of the Day ———————————————— MR 2.0

Which jar has more marbles?
How can you tell?

Number Sense ———————————————————— NS 1.2

Calendar ——————————————————————— NS 1.1

Numerical Fluency ——————————————————— NS 1.2

5, 17, 33, 41, 26

Use with text pp. 263A–264

Read a Calendar

Problem of the Day ———————————————— NS 3.0

Do you see more than 10 or less than 10 cars?

Measurement and Geometry ———————————— MG 2.1

What has four straight sides but is not a square?

Number of the Day ———————————————— NS 1.2

Numerical Fluency ———————————————— NS 1.2

1	3	5	7	9
2	4	6	8	10

Name _____

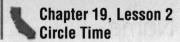

Times of Day

Problem of the Day ———————————— MG 1.3

Sunday comes before Monday.
Monday comes before Tuesday.
What day comes before Wednesday?

Measurement and Geometry ——————— MG 1.1

On your mat, draw the one you think holds more.

Workmat 1

Words of the Day ———————————— KEY MG 1.0

| before | after |

Numerical Fluency ———————————— NS 1.2

Name _____

Days of the Week

Problem of the Day ——————————— MG 1.2

Which of these would you see at night?

Statistics, Data Analysis, and Probability ——————— KEY SDAP 1.2

1   2   2   1   2   2

Number of the Day ——————————— NS 1.2

8

Numerical Fluency ——————————— NS 1.2

5   10   15   20   25   30   35   40   45   50

Name _____

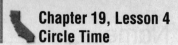

Months of the Year

Problem of the Day ———————————————— MG 1.3

Which day is missing?

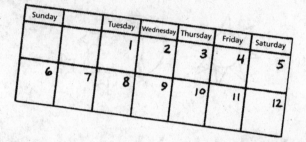

Number Sense ———————————————————— NS 1.1

Which plate has more?

Calendar ———————————————————————— MG 1.2

On what day do you think next month will start?

Numerical Fluency ————————————————— NS 1.2

20 21 22 23 24 25 26 27 28 29 30

Name _____

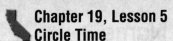

Use a Picture

Problem of the Day ———————————————— MG 1.2

Which month comes before March? Which month comes after?

_____ March _____

Number Sense ———————————————— NS 2.0

Workmat 1

$$7 - 3 = 4$$

Word of the Day ———————————————— NS 3.0

estimate

Are there about 10 chairs in the room or about 20? Estimate the number. Count to find out.

Numerical Fluency ———————————————— NS 1.1

Are we wearing more long sleeves or short sleeves?

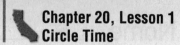
Hours and Minutes

Problem of the Day ———————————— MG 1.2

What day of the week is May 16th on this calendar?

			May			
Sun.	Mon.	Tue.	Wed.	Thu.	Fri.	Sat.
			1	2	3	4
5	6	7	8	9	10	11
12	13	14	15	16	17	18
19	20	21	22	23	24	25
26	27	28	29	30	31	

Number Sense ———————————— NS 1.3

10

Calendar ———————————— MG 1.2

Numerical Fluency ———————————— NS 1.2

Use with text pp. 290A–290D

Name _____

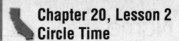

Estimate with Time

Problem of the Day ———————————— KEY **MG 1.0**

Which activity takes about a minute?

Measurement and Geometry ——————— MG 2.0

Words of the Day ————————————— MG 2.2

| top |

| bottom |

Numerical Fluency ————————————— NS 1.2

10 11 12 13 14 15 16 17 18 19

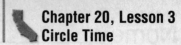
Time to the Hour

Problem of the Day ———————————— KEY

Jenna built two stacks of coins.
Which stack took about one minute to build?

Statistics, Data Analysis, and Probability ———————— KEY SDAP 1.2

Number of the Day ———————————— MG 1.2

| 12 |

Numerical Fluency ———————————— NS 1.2

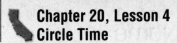
Relate Time to Events

Problem of the Day ———————————————— MG 1.2

What time does the clock show?

Number Sense ———————————————— NS 1.3

Calendar ———————————————— MG 1.4

Class Schedule	
8:00 - 9:00	Math
9:00 - 10:00	Spelling
10:00 - 11:00	Reading
11:00 - 11:15	Recess

Numerical Fluency ———————————————— KEY NS 1.0

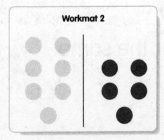

Workmat 2

Name _____

Act It Out

Problem of the Day ———————————— MG 1.2

This afternoon Jack will plant some flowers.
Which clock shows what time he will plant the flowers?

Measurement and Geometry ———————— MG 1.2

Look at the class calendar.
If yesterday was [Tuesday], what day is tomorrow?

Word of the Day ———————————— NS 1.2

third

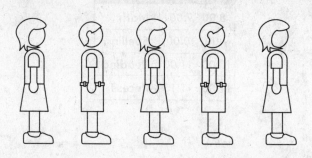

Numerical Fluency ———————————— NS 1.1

Tell which is more, less, or the same.

Name _____

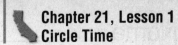

Twenty

Problem of the Day ———————————— MG 1.2

Luke started to read at 3:00.
He finished reading at 4:00.
For how long did Luke read?

Number Sense ———————————— KEY NS 2.1

Write a number sentence to show how many rocks in all.

Word of the Day ———————————— NS 2.0

subtract

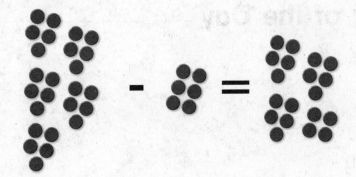

Numerical Fluency ———————————— KEY NS 1.0

15 is 10 and 5

Numbers 21–25

Problem of the Day —————————— NS 1.2

20 is ___ tens.

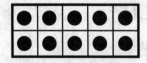

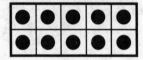

Measurement and Geometry ————— MG 2.1

Number of the Day —————————— KEY NS 1.0

14

14 = 7 + 7
14 = 10 + 4

Numerical Fluency —————————— NS 1.2

Find groups of 10.

Numbers 26–30

Problem of the Day ————————— NS 1.2

How many more cubes do we need to make 23?

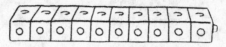
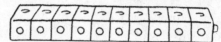

Measurement and Geometry ————————— MG 1.2

Calendar ——————————————————— MG 1.2

Numerical Fluency ———————————————— NS 1.2

Name _____

Order Numbers 0–30

Problem of the Day ———————————— NS 1.2

It is more than 26.
It is less than 28.
What is the number?

26 28

Measurement and Geometry ———————— MG 2.1

Number of the Day ———————————— MG 1.2

30

April						
Sun.	Mon.	Tue.	Wed.	Thu.	Fri.	Sat.
			1	2	3	4
5	6	7	8	9	10	11
12	13	14	15	16	17	18
19	20	21	22	23	24	25
26	27	28	29	30		

Numerical Fluency ———————————— NS 1.2

1 2 3 4 5 6 7 8 9 10

Use with text pp. 314A–314D

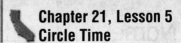
Reasonable Answers

Problem of the Day ——————————————— NS 1.2

Mia dropped some paint on her number card.
Which card did she drop the paint on?

20 21 22 23 ● 25 26 27 28 29 30

Measurement and Geometry ——————— MG 1.3

Calendar ————————————————————— MR 2.0

Do you think the last Wednesday in the month has a date that is
more than, less than, or exactly 15?

Numerical Fluency ————————————————— NS 1.2

Count using teamwork!

Name _____

Estimate

Problem of the Day ——————————— NS 3.1

Do you see more than 25 or less than 25?

Number Sense ——————————— NS 2.0

4   5   9

Calendar ——————————————— NS 1.2

Numerical Fluency ——————————— NS 1.2

Use with text pp. 320A–320D

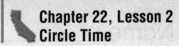
Estimation

Problem of the Day ———————————————— NS 1.1

Which jar has more marbles?
How can you tell?

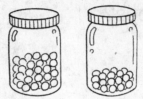

Statistics, Data Analysis, and Probability ———————————— KEY SDAP 1.2

Word of the Day ———————————————————— MG 1.3

Monday

January						
Sun.	Mon.	Tue.	Wed.	Thu.	Fri.	Sat.
			1	2	3	4
5	6	7	8	9	10	11
12	13	14	15	16	17	18
19	20	21	22	23	24	25
26	27	28	29	30	31	

Numerical Fluency ———————————————————— NS 1.2

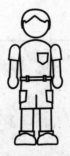

Name _____

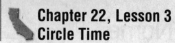
Compare Quantities

Problem of the Day ————————————— NS 1.3

Which has more cubes?
How can you tell?

Number Sense ————————————————— NS 3.0

Number of the Day ————————————— NS 1.2

| 19 |

19

Numerical Fluency ———————————— NS 1.2

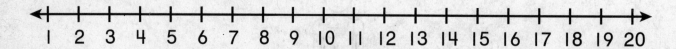

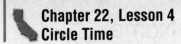
Calendar: Use Numbers 1–31

Problem of the Day ———————————— NS 1.3

Which group has less?

Algebra and Functions ———————————— KEY AF 1.1

Which shape does not belong?
Why?

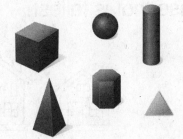

Calendar ———————————————————— MG 1.2

Numerical Fluency ——————————————— NS 1.2

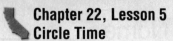
Use Logical Thinking

Problem of the Day ——————————— NS 1.2

What numbers are likely to go in the boxes?

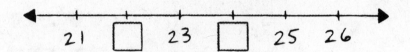

Measurement and Geometry ——————— MG 1.1

Circle the house that is tallest.

Word of the Day ————————————— MG 1.2

yesterday

What did you do yesterday?

Numerical Fluency ———————————— NS 1.2

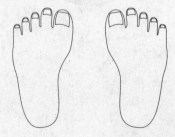

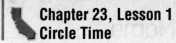
Solids

Problem of the Day ————————————————— NS 1.2

I am thinking of a number.

It is less than 16.

It is more than 10.

Which number could it be?

6   12   25

Number Sense ——————————————————— NS 1.2

Which animal is first? second? third? fourth?

Calendar ————————————————————————— MG 1.2

Numerical Fluency ——————————————— NS 1.2

9   12   5   3   8   11   13   6   1   7   14   10   2   15   4

Sort Solids

Problem of the Day ——————— MG 2.1

How are they alike? How are they different?

Number Sense ——————— NS 1.1

Number of the Day ——————— NS 1.2

What do you know about zero?

Numerical Fluency ——————— NS 1.1

Are there 30 in our class? more? fewer?

Name _____

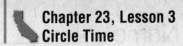
Combine and Separate Plane Shapes

Problem of the Day ———————————— MG 2.1

I can slide.
I cannot roll.
What am I?

Measurement and Geometry ———————— MG 2.2

Word of the Day ———————————— KEY SDAP 1.2

pattern

Numerical Fluency ———————————— NS 1.2

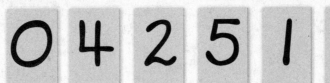

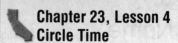
Combine and Separate Solid Shapes

Problem of the Day ———————————— MR 1.2

Number Sense ———————————————— MG 1.4

What do you usually do at 12:00 in the afternoon?

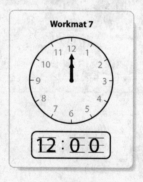

clock

Word of the Day ——————————————— MG 2.1

triangle

Which shapes do not belong with the others?

Numerical Fluency ——————————————— NS 1.2

20 21 22 23 24 25 26 27 28 29 30

Circle Time

112

Use with text pp. 347A–348

Use Logical Reasoning

Problem of the Day ——————————————— MG 2.2

Which of these could you use to build a tower?

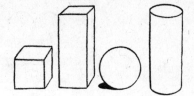

Number Sense ——————————————— NS 1.2

Please giggle if you are tenth.

Word of the Day ——————————————— MG 1.1

corner

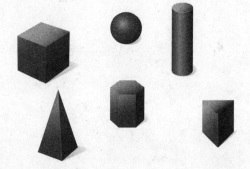

Numerical Fluency ——————————————— NS 1.2

17 14 19 13 15 12 11 18 16

Name _____

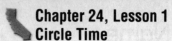
Compare Length

Problem of the Day ———————————— MG 2.1

How many circles do you see?

Algebra and Functions ———————————— AF 1.0

What is the same about all of these?
What is different?

Calendar ———————————————— MG 1.2

Numerical Fluency ———————————— NS 1.2

Sort by Length

Problem of the Day ————————————————— MG 1.1

Which leash is longer?

Measurement and Geometry ——————————— MG 1.1

Name something that is longer than this ribbon.

Words of the Day ———————————————————— NS 2.0

| add | subtract |

Would we add or subtract?

Numerical Fluency ——————————————————— NS 1.2

Are there more Ss or Ts in the names?

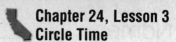

Compare Weights

Problem of the Day ———————————————— MG 1.1

Put these in order from shortest to longest.

Measurement and Geometry ———————————— MG 2.0

Number of the Day ————————————————— NS 3.0

20

Are there 20 children in the room, more, or fewer?
Count to check.

Numerical Fluency ————————————————— NS 1.2

Name _____

Compare Capacity

Problem of the Day ———————————————— MG 1.1

Which of these objects would be harder to carry? Tell why.

Number Sense ————————————————————— NS 2.0

Would we add or subtract to find how many are left?

Word of the Day ————————————————— MG 1.2

morning

Numerical Fluency ——————————————— KEY NS 1.0

Use with text pp. 358E–358H

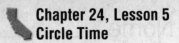
Use Logical Reasoning

Problem of the Day ———————————————— MG 2.2

What different ways might we sort the containers?

Algebra and Functions ———————————————— AF 1.0

Word of the Day ———————————————— MG 1.1

longer

Numerical Fluency ———————————————— NS 1.2

22 23 25 26 27

Circle Time
118
Use with text pp. 359A–360

Looking Ahead Activities

These activities will help you
get ready for math next year.

Name _____ Date _____

Numbers Through 50

CA Standards
NS 1.2; prepares for Grade 1
KEY NS 1.1

| **By yourself** |
| **Materials:** connecting cubes |

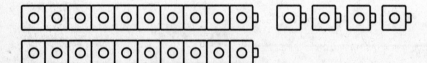

_____
__ __
_____

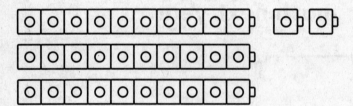

_____
__ __
_____

_____
__ __
_____

_____
__ __
_____

Directions: Use connecting cubes to show the same number of cubes.
Count how many. Write the number.

Objective: Read, count, and recognize numbers to 50.

Name _____

Count on a Hundred Chart

You can count on a hundred chart.

CA Standards
NS 1.2; prepares for Grade 1
KEY NS 1.1

By yourself

1	2	3	4	5	6	7	8	9	10
11	12	13	14	15	16	17	18	19	20
21	22	23	24	25	26	27	28	29	30
31	32	33	34	35	36	37	38	39	40
41	42	43	44	45	46	47	48	49	50
51	52	53	54	55	56	57	58	59	60
61	62	63	64	65	66	67	68	69	70
71	72	73	74	75	76	77	78	79	80
81	82	83	84	85	86	87	88	89	90
91	92	93	94	95	96	97	98	99	100

Count 18, 19, 20, 21

1 ⭐ 7, 8, 9, _____ _____ _____

2 🍃 12, 13, 14, _____ _____ _____

3 🍎 19, 20, 21, _____ _____ _____

4 🌸 78, 79, 80, _____ _____ _____

5 🌲 37, 38, 39, _____ _____ _____

6 🦋 50, 51, 52, _____ _____ _____

Directions: Count. Use the hundred chart. Write the numbers.

Objective: Read, count, and recognize numbers to 100 on a hundred chart.

Name _____ Date _____

Count by 10s

You can count by 10s on a hundred chart.

CA Standards
NS 1.2; prepares for Grade 1
KEY NS 2.4

With your group

1	2	3	4	5	6	7	8	9	
11	12	13	14	15	16	17	18	19	
21	22	23	24	25	26	27	28	29	
31	32	33	34	35	36	37	38	39	
41	42	43	44	45	46	47	48	49	
51	52	53	54	55	56	57	58	59	
61	62	63	64	65	66	67	68	69	
71	72	73	74	75	76	77	78	79	
81	82	83	84	85	86	87	88	89	
91	92	93	94	95	96	97	98	99	

Directions: Write the numbers that are missing from the hundred chart.
Count by 10s.

Objective: Count by 10s on a hundred chart.

3

Name _____

Count by 2s and 5s

1	2	3	4	5	6	7	8	9	10
11	12	13	14	15	16	17	18	19	20
21	22	23	24	25	26	27	28	29	30
31	32	33	34	35	36	37	38	39	40
41	42	43	44	45	46	47	48	49	50

CA Standards
NS 1.2; prepares for Grade 1
KEY NS 2.4

With your partner

Materials:
5-part spinner labeled 2, 4, 6, 8, 10, and Spinner A; 6-part spinner labeled 5, 10, 15, 20, 25, 30, and Spinner B; counting chips in two colors

Count by 2s and 5s Game

Score Card 1 – Count by 2s

	Player 1	Player 2
1		
2		

Score Card 2 – Count by 5s

	Player 1	Player 2
1		
2		

Directions: Take turns with a partner. Spin Spinner A. Count by 2s on the hundred chart. Write your number on the score card. Circle the greater number. Spin Spinner B. Count by 5s on the hundred chart. Write your number on the score card. Circle the greater number.

Objective: Count by 2s and 5s.

Value of Coins

CA Standards
prepares for Grade 1 NS 1.5

With your partner

Materials:
pennies, nickels, dimes

penny	nickel	dime
1 cent	5 cents	10 cents
1¢	5¢	10¢

1

_____ _____ _____ _____ _____ _____ = _____ ¢

____¢ ____¢ ____¢ ____¢ ____¢ ____¢

2

_____ _____ _____ = _____ ¢

____¢ ____¢ ____¢

3

_____ _____ _____ _____ _____ = _____ ¢

____¢ ____¢ ____¢ ____¢ ____¢

Directions: Use coins. Count to find the total amount. Count pennies by 1s.
Count nickels by 5s. Count dimes by 10s. Write the amount.

Objective: Find the value of sets of pennies, nickels, or dimes.

Name _____

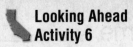

Nickels and Pennies

CA Standards
Prepares for Grade 1
KEY NS 2.4

With your partner

Materials:
pennies, nickels

_ _ ¢   _ _ ¢   _ _ ¢   _ _ ¢   _ _ ¢

Total Value: ____ ¢

_ _ ¢   _ _ ¢   _ _ ¢   _ _ ¢

Total Value: ____ ¢

_ _ ¢   _ _ ¢   _ _ ¢   _ _ ¢   _ _ ¢

Total Value: ____ ¢

_ _ ¢   _ _ ¢   _ _ ¢   _ _ ¢   _ _ ¢   _ _ ¢

Total Value: ____ ¢

Directions: Use coins. Count on nickels by 5s. Count on pennies by 1s. Write
the total amount.

Objective: Find the value of sets of nickels and pennies.

Name _____ Date _____

Add Pennies

CA Standards
NS 2.0; prepares for Grade 1
NS 1.5, **KEY** NS 2.1, **KEY** NS 2.5

With your partner

Materials:
pennies

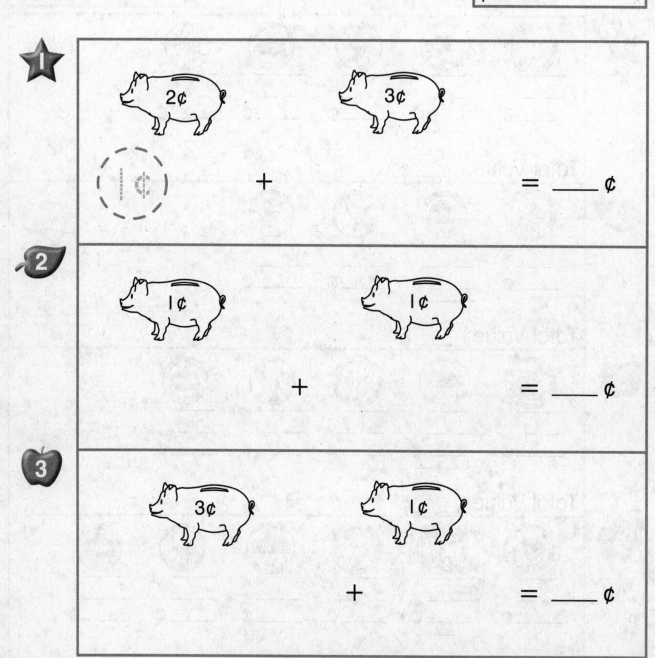

Directions 1-3: Show the pennies for each bank. Trace them. Add. Write how many in all.

Objective: Model addition facts with sums to 10.

Subtract Pennies

CA Standards
NS 2.0; prepares for Grade 1
NS 1.5, **KEY** NS 2.1, **KEY** NS 2.5

With your class

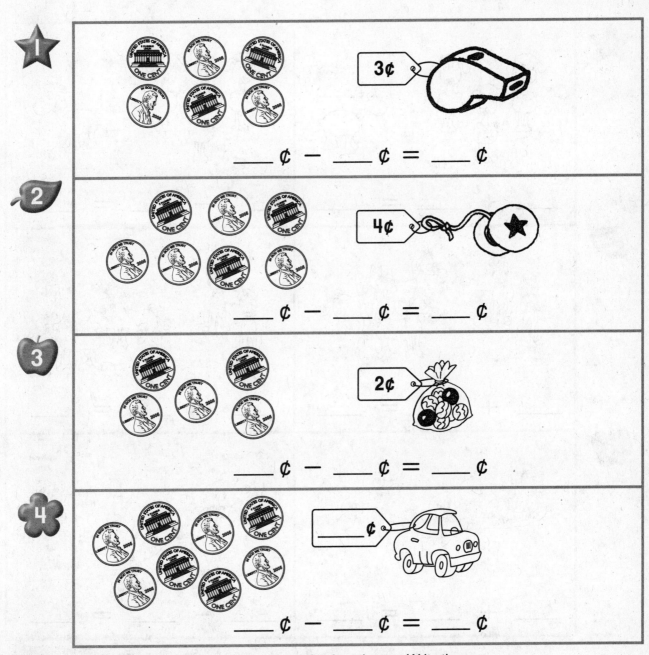

1 3¢

___ ¢ − ___ ¢ = ___ ¢

2 4¢

___ ¢ − ___ ¢ = ___ ¢

3 2¢

___ ¢ − ___ ¢ = ___ ¢

4 ___¢

___ ¢ − ___ ¢ = ___ ¢

Directions: 1–3. Cross out the pennies you need to buy the toy. Write the subtraction sentence that tells how many are left. **4.** Write a price for the toy less than 8¢. Cross out the pennies and write a subtraction sentence.

Objective: Subtract from 10 or less.

Name _____ Date _____

Relate Addition and Subtraction

With your partner

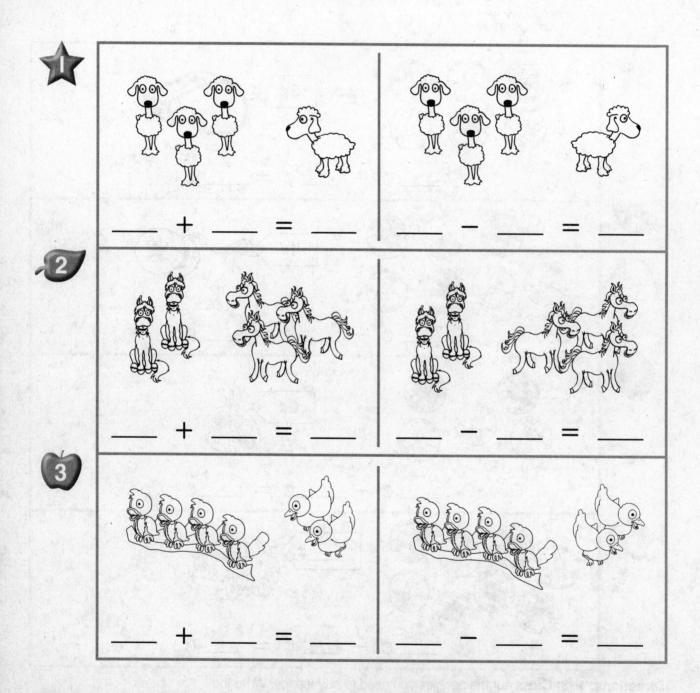

Directions: Add. Write the addition sentence. Then subtract. Write the subtraction sentence.

Objective: Relate addition and subtraction.

9

Name _____

Choose the Operation

CA Standards
NS 2.0; prepares for Grade 1
KEY NS 2.2

With your partner

1. $5 \bigcirc 2 = \underline{\hspace{1cm}}$

2. $4 \bigcirc 4 = \underline{\hspace{1cm}}$

3. $10 \bigcirc 3 = \underline{\hspace{1cm}}$

Directions: 1–3. Tell your partner a story about each picture. Complete the
number sentence.

Objective: Choose addition or subtraction to solve a problem.

Name _____ Date _____

Order Length

CA Standards
KEY MG 1.0, MG 1.1; prepares
for Grade 1 MG 1.0, MG 1.1

With your group

Materials:
classroom objects

Shortest		Longest
⭐ 1		
🍃 2		
🍎 3		
🌸 4		

Directions: 1–4. Choose 3 classroom objects. Compare with your group.
Draw the objects from shortest to longest.

Objective: Compare and order objects using length.

Name _____

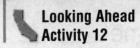

Measure Length

CA Standards
MG 1.1; prepares for Grade 1
MG 1.1

With your partner

Materials:
connecting cubes

⭐ 1

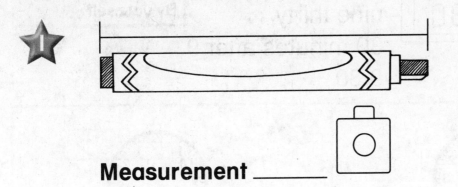

Measurement _____

🍃 2

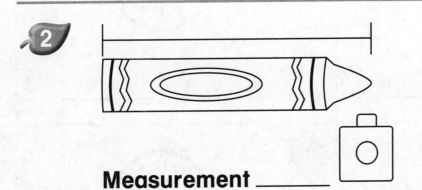

Measurement _____

🍎 3

Measurement _____

🌸 4

Measurement _____

Directions: Measure the length or height in cubes. Record the length.

Objective: Use cubes to measure the length or height of objects.

Looking Ahead

12

Name _____ Date _____

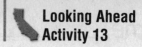
Time to the Half-Hour

  nine thirty
30 minutes after 9
9:30

CA Standards
MG 1.4; prepares for Grade 1
MG 1.2

By yourself

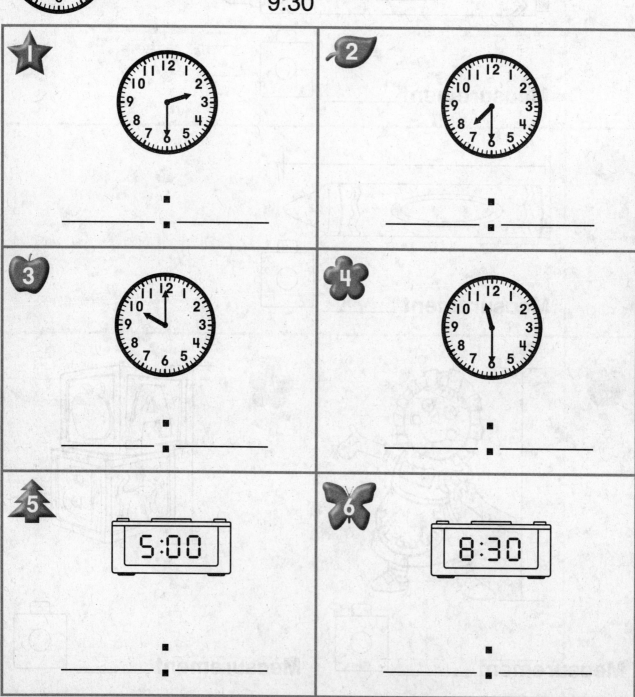

Directions: 1–6. Write the time shown on the clock.

Objective: Read time to the half-hour on analog and digital clocks.

Name _____

Sort Plane Shapes

CA Standards
MG 2.1, MG 2.2; prepares for
Grade 1 MG 2.1, MG 2.2

By yourself

Directions: **1.** Draw the shapes that have curves. **2.** Draw the shapes with 4 sides.
3. Draw the shapes with 3 corners.

Objective: Sort two-dimensional shapes.

Name _____ Date _____

Faces of
Three-Dimensional Objects

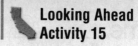

CA Standards
MG 2.2; prepares for Grade 1
MG 2.1, MG 2.2

With your group

Materials:
three-dimensional shapes

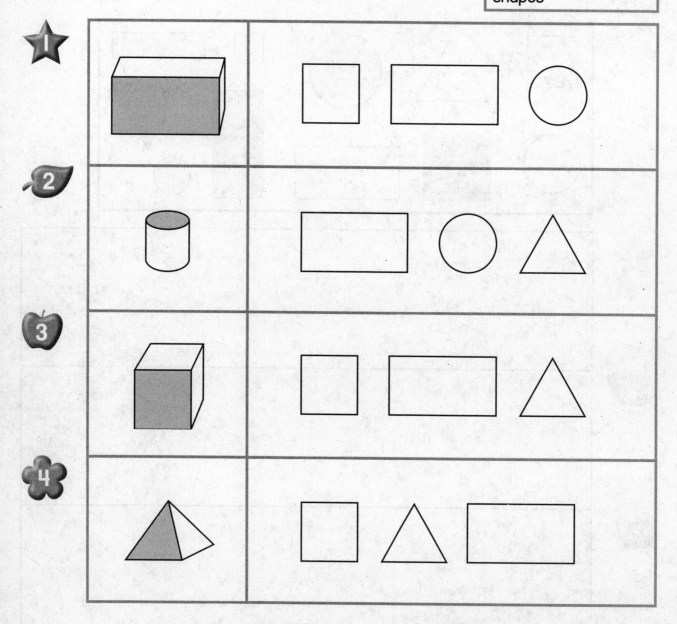

Directions: 1–4. Look at the gray surface of the three-dimensional shape. Circle the matching two-dimensional shape.

Objective: Identify the surfaces of three-dimensional shapes.

Name _____

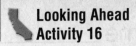

Extend Patterns

CA Standards
KEY SDAP 1.2; prepares for
Grade 1 **KEY** SDAP 2.1

With your partner

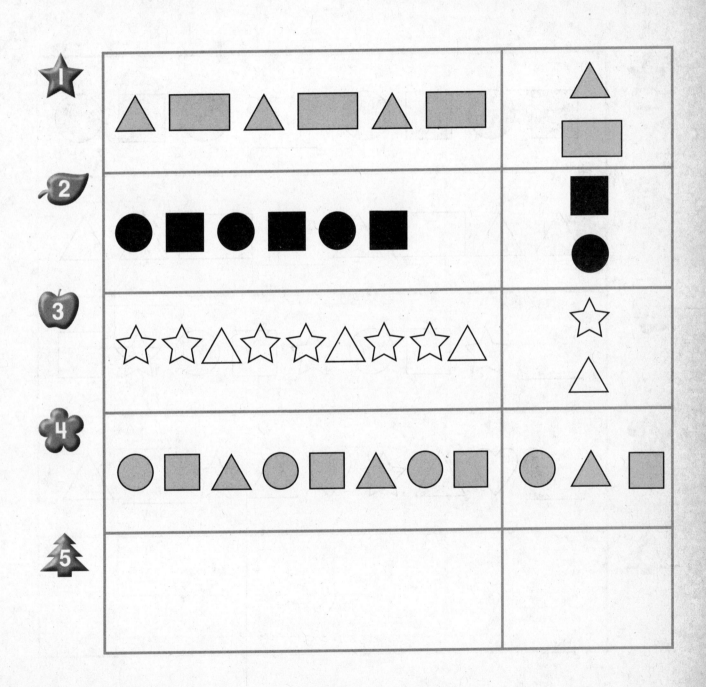

Directions: 1–4. Circle the figure that most likely comes next.

5. Draw your own repeating pattern.

Objective: Extend repeating patterns.

Name _____ Date _____

What's Missing?

CA Standards
KEY SDAP 1.2; prepares for
Grade 1 KEY SDAP 2.1

With your partner

Directions: 1–4. Draw the missing shape in the pattern. **5.** Draw your own pattern with a missing shape. Ask your partner to complete your pattern.

Objective: Identify the missing part of a pattern.

Name _____

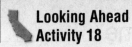
Number Patterns

CA Standards
KEY SDAP 1.2; prepares for
Grade 1 KEY SDAP 2.1

By yourself

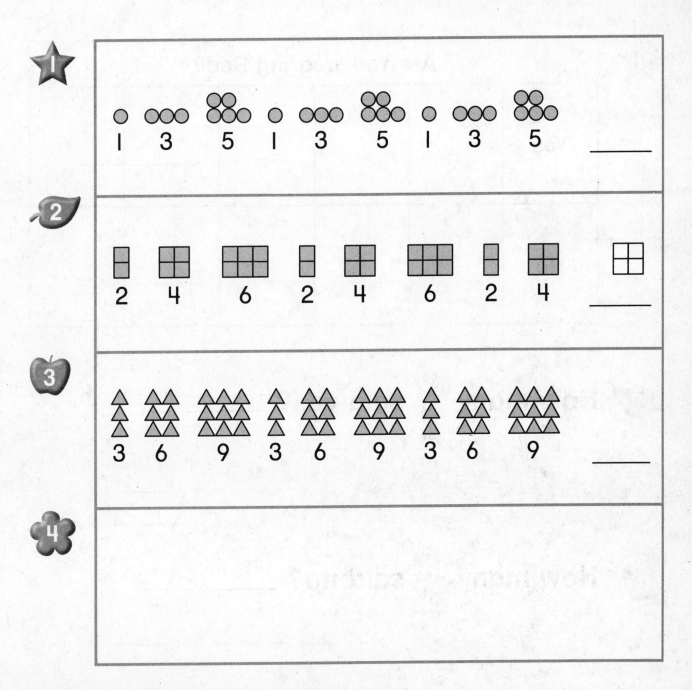

1
1   3   5   1   3   5   1   3   5   _____

2
2   4   6   2   4   6   2   4   _____

3
3   6   9   3   6   9   3   6   9   _____

4

Directions: **1–3.** Write the number that most likely comes next.
4. Write your own number pattern.

Objective: Extend number patterns.

Name _____ Date _____

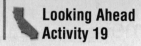
Make a Tally Chart

CA Standards
SDAP 1.1; prepares for Grade 1
SDAP 1.2

With your partner

Are You Wearing Red?					
Yes					
No					

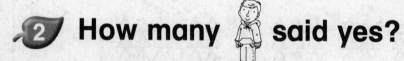

2 How many said yes? _____

3 How many said no? _____

Directions: 1. Ask 5 friends if they are wearing red. Make 1 tally for each answer.
2–3. Use the tally chart.

Objective: Make a tally chart.

Name _____

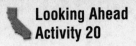
Use a Graph

CA Standards
SDAP 1.1; prepares for Grade 1
SDAP 1.2

With your class

Directions: 1. Circle the one the most children chose. 2. Circle the one the fewest children chose. 3. Circle the one that 5 children chose. 4. Circle the one that 7 children chose.

Objective: Use information from a graph to answer questions.